Treasurer's House

NOTICE
All Workmen are
requested to wear
Slippers when work-
ing in this House.
by Order
FRANK GREEN

York

National
Trust

Period Rooms for a Personal Collection

The rooms you will walk round today were the work of one man – Frank Green – a wealthy Yorkshire collector who bought Treasurer's House in 1897. He was a bachelor and never intended the place to be a cosy home. Instead, he created a series of period rooms as an appropriate setting for his fine collection of antique furniture, specifying exactly where each piece should stand with stud-marks in the floor.

The building itself has a much longer history. Treasurer's House stands on the site of the mansion of the medieval Treasurers of York Minster. In 1547, at the time of the Reformation, the office of Treasurer was abolished, and, as a result of later rebuilding, the name is virtually all that survives of the medieval building. Although the earliest section of the present house dates from Elizabethan times, the Young family, who bought it in 1565, rebuilt the main part of the house in the early 17th century, creating the present garden front with its twin Dutch gables and classical central entrance. Thomas Young sold up in 1648 during the Civil War, and thereafter the house passed through many hands: it was eventually subdivided and began to fall into decay.

Between 1897 and 1900 Frank Green and his architect, Temple Moore, restored the exterior to something like its original shape by demolishing incongruous extensions added in the 19th century. Over the years, Green continually changed and rearranged the furniture and added to the decoration and fittings as his ideas about particular rooms developed. He had long opened his house to the public and on his retirement to Somerset in 1930 he gave Treasurer's House with its contents to the National Trust. It was thus the first historic house to be acquired by the Trust complete with its contents.

The English 'love-seat' of *c.*1730 in the Tapestry Room still has its original needlework upholstery

Frank Green in hunting pink; painted by J.R.G. Exley (South Dressing Room)

The King's Room – one of the 'period rooms' created by Frank Green

Tour of the House

The Lobby

19th-century Delft tiles in the Kitchen

During the 1990s a major programme of redecoration took place in the public rooms as part of a policy of returning the house to its appearance in 1930, when it was given to the Trust by Frank Green. During the 1960s and '70s the Trust policy of trying to give the house an 18th-century character had led to the painting-out of many of the earlier schemes. Room contents have also been mostly restored to their 1930 positions. *Wherever possible, the furniture and pictures are described clockwise from the entrance door.*

The Lobby
This was added to the house in 1906. The 18th-century doorcases and probably the cornice came from Micklegate House in York. Green's dark grained woodwork and stone-coloured walls were reintroduced in 1993.

FURNITURE

Joined oak chest, English, second half of 17th century.

PICTURE

Frank Green by J.R.G. Exley, 1935.

The Entrance Hall
This room dates back to the early 17th century, and the fireplace is contemporary. Green replaced the pair of 18th-century sash-windows overlooking the garden with 17th-century-style mullions and transoms, and introduced the windows overlooking the back yard. The current decoration, copied from the design found underneath 17th-century panelling at Clifton House in King's Lynn, Norfolk, was introduced before 1922. The pinnacle decoration above the frieze, which had been painted out in the 1970s, was reintroduced in 1991.

FURNITURE

Mahogany elbow chair, English, c.1770.

Longcase clock, with floral marquetry, late 17th-century. Movement by Ben Merriman, London.

Teak 'Burgomaster' chair, Dutch colonial, south India or Sri Lanka, late 17th-century.

Pier-glass with verre eglomisé (painted glass) borders, English, c.1710.

Console table in the Palladian style, English, 19th-century.

Barometer by B. Storr of York, late 18th-century.

Oak gate-leg table, English, late 17th- or early 18th-century.

Walnut buffet à deux corps (two-part sideboard), French, c.1650.

Walnut and elm tea-table, English, c.1750. One half of the top has been lost and the rear gates removed.

PICTURE

Treasurer's House in the mid-18th century. This shows the sash-windows removed by Frank Green.

The Kitchen
The lobby includes a display of photographs of Frank Green and his staff and a watercolour of Green's engineering works at Wakefield by J.E. Grace, 1873. Frank Green's Kitchen was restored only in 1997 after use as a flat and shop. The 19th-century hand-painted Delft tiles and kitchen spit were introduced by Green, but the range is a re-creation designed to fit within the 17th-century chimneypiece. With no precise evidence of how the Kitchen was laid out, it has been furnished with appropriate pieces. The Scullery beyond is used for art exhibitions.

The Entrance Hall

An ebony chair from south-east India, *c.*1680–1720 (West Sitting Room)

The West Sitting Room

This room went through an extraordinary number of changes during Frank Green's ownership. Initially, the two windows overlooking the lawn were converted from sash to mullion and transom and the third window introduced or reopened. The chimneypiece with the gilded figure of Leda and the Swan was moved from an 18th-century panelled room on the ground floor of the current Hall. An alcove to its right was taken in from the Entrance Hall and given a classical open pediment above a display case. Sometime before 1910 the room was partitioned off to create a corridor between the Entrance Hall and the Hall, thus leaving the chimneypiece oddly off-centre. The current panelling was introduced during the 1920s and the closet created at the same time.

FURNITURE

Four ebony chairs, Dutch colonial, Coromandel coast, south-east India, 1680–1720.

Walnut fold-over writing-table, English, *c.*1700.

Yew wood gate-leg table, early 18th-century.

Model of the South African War Memorial in Duncombe Place, York, designed by G.F. Bodley.

Ivory tripod games table, Murshidabad, north-east India, *c.*1800.

Pair of ivory chairs, Murshidabad, *c.*1800.

PICTURES

A Female Tepidarium, in the manner of the Fontainebleau School, 16th-century.

Female Nude, attributed to the York artist William Etty (1787–1849).

Peter the Great, after an engraving of a picture by Jacopo Amigoni (*c.*1682–1752) in the Winter Palace, St Petersburg.

The West Sitting Room in 1902

The West Sitting Room in 1922

The West Sitting Room in 1910

6

Dutch Kitchen Scene; by Joachim Beuckelaer (Hall)

(*Below*) The Hall

The Hall

Frank Green's most radical remodelling of the house was the creation of this 'medieval' great hall, which he was convinced had been an original feature. Between 1897 and 1900 existing divisions, panelling and an upper floor were all removed, and the 18th-century sash-windows replaced by mullions and transoms. In fact, much of the existing structure dates only from the 16th and 17th centuries, and the steps at the south end represent the different levels of a 16th-century range now occupied by the Dining Room and West Sitting Room. A Jacobean frieze was uncovered at the other end of the room and the fireplace raised to what Green claimed was the original floor level. The staircase was based on one at St William's College, York, but it was embellished by 1922 with relief ornament copied from Knole in Kent. The head known as Queen Philippa, now above the garden door, was found in the basement.

FURNITURE

Pair of ebonised beechwood elbow chairs, English, *c.*1700.

Oak table, English, *c.*1600. The top is made from a single tree, cut down the middle into two planks.

Jansenist crucifix of pearwood, ebony and tortoiseshell.

Walnut and cane elbow chair, English, *c.*1685.

Small pine table with oak top, English, *c.*1660–80.

Walnut and cane elbow chair, English, *c.*1715.

Two joined oak great chairs, English, mid-17th-century.

Oak gate-leg table in original condition, English, late 17th-century.

Pair of upholstered chairs with walnut frames, English, *c.*1700. Ex-Rushbrooke Hall, Suffolk.

Four painted oak stools, *c.*1700.

Joined oak great chair, English, probably Yorkshire, *c.*1660–80.

Oak table and benches, the table dated 1686 and with the initials of the owner, William Cass of Peep O'Day Farm, Easingwold, Yorkshire.

PICTURES

Charles II, after Adriaen Hannemann (*c.*1604–71).

Charles I, a copy of the painting by Van Dyck in the Louvre.

The Road to Calvary, 16th-century Flemish School (on loan from York City Art Gallery).

Portrait of a Boy, style of Edward Bower, *c.*1640.

Dutch Kitchen Scene, by Joachim Beuckelaer (*c.*1530–73).

The Blue Drawing Room

This was the principal room in the north-west wing of the house, which was heavily remodelled in the late 17th century. The ceiling of that date survives, but during the 18th century the space was divided into two separate panelled rooms. These were initially retained by Frank Green and furnished as a Queen Anne drawing room and a Restoration room. About 1910, the partition wall was removed and the doorcases and panelling reordered. The chimneypiece from the smaller drawing room, based on a published design by Batty Langley of 1739, was re-centred in the enlarged room. The current decoration of peacock blue with bronze picking-out matches that which Frank Green always retained. It had been replaced by the Trust in 1968 with a scheme of off-whites which survived until 1999.

FURNITURE

Pair of giltwood girandoles (wall-lights) in the baroque style, 19th-century.

Set of four walnut chairs with needlework covers, English, *c*.1725.

Carved and painted table in the Palladian style, 19th-century (?).

Japanned cabinet on a later carved giltwood stand.

Pair of giltwood pier-glasses, English, *c*.1720.

Pair of Boulle cabinets from Cassiobury Park, Hertfordshire, French, 19th-century.

Boulle desk, French, 19th-century.

Three carved giltwood console tables, French or English, *c*.1755, from Mexborough House, London.

Pair of Chippendale revival giltwood girandoles, English, 19th-century.

Giltwood pier-glass carved in the rococo style, English, 19th-century.

Pair of carved giltwood pier-glasses in the Palladian style, English, *c*.1730.

Pair of carved giltwood torchères, English, *c*.1715. The monogram on the top is that of John Churchill, 1st Duke of Marlborough. Presumably made for Blenheim by a leading English maker, perhaps James Moore.

Pair of oak and parcel gilt console tables, French, *c*.1720.

Pole-screen of 18th-century needlework on a giltwood base, of *c*.1830.

Suite of carved and gilt seat furniture, English, *c*.1790, in the French style.

Boulle writing-table, French, *c*.1715. The marquetry depicts scenes from the Comédie Italienne.

PICTURE

Portrait of a Lady, English School, 17th-century.

Detail of the inlay on the 19th-century Boulle desk in the Blue Drawing Room

(*Below*) The Blue Drawing Room

The Napoleonic ship
model in the Court Room

Two Dutch Children;
painted in 1629 (Court
Room)

The Court Room

This is part of the 17th-century north-west wing of the house, and the fireplace (which Green wrongly considered to be Tudor), overmantel, plastered beams and cornice survive from that period. Green introduced the current window, which replaced a doorway, and divided the room, with the window side containing a back staircase and lavatory and the fireplace side a cloakroom. The latter was hung with a Watts & Co. wallpaper – 'Pear' pattern – which survives behind the existing panelling introduced before 1922. Green's decoration of that period was reintroduced in 1996.

FURNITURE

Four walnut chairs, English, *c.*1735. The tapestry covers are possibly from the Mortlake or Soho workshops.

A made-up walnut cabinet. The upper part is from an English desk-and-bookcase, *c.*1730.

George III triple chair-back settee.

Late 17th-century Japanese lacquered cabinet on a japanned stand in the George III style.

Model of a ship of the line made by French prisoners at the time of the Napoleonic Wars, probably from bone and whalebone. The rigging was renewed in the 1920s. The case stands on a late 17th- or early 18th-century Spanish walnut table.

PICTURES

Mary Earnshaw, wife of John Green, copy by Mrs Basil Hall of an early 18th-century portrait.

Joseph Green, copy by Mrs Basil Hall of an early 18th-century portrait.

Portrait of a Man, Dutch School, 1631.

Two Dutch Children, Dutch School, 1629.

Lakeland Scene, by Charles Towne (1763–1842).

The William and Mary Staircase

This has been relatively little altered since it was created in the early 18th century. Green restored the ground-floor Venetian window (which had been turned into a doorway in the 19th century), inserted the adjacent mullioned-and-transomed windows on both ground and first floors, blocked up doors on the landing, and introduced new cornices. Green always decorated the room with Watts & Co.'s 'Malmesbury' pattern paper, which was reprinted in the correct colourways in 1995, using the original pearwood blocks still owned by Watts & Co.

FURNITURE

Slab table with walnut and parcel-gilt frame and pink marble top from Apethorpe Hall, Northamptonshire, English, *c.*1725.

Eagle console table in an early 18th-century style.

Carved giltwood mirror in the style of the Bookers of Dublin.

Mahogany corner chair, English, *c.*1760.

Carved and gilt chest or *cassone* of sarcophagus form, English, *c.*1730.

Carved and gilded chair, English, *c.*1695.

PICTURES

Portrait of an Unknown Lady (despite the label identifying her as Mme Necker), French School, early 18th-century.

Portrait of a Lady, English School, late 18th-century.

Prince Charles Louis, after Van Dyck.

Three portraits of members of the Beaumont family of Whitley Beaumont, English School, *c.*1740.

The William and Mary Staircase

The Upper Landing

FURNITURE

Set of four mahogany chairs, English, *c.*1760.
All these chairs have been reduced in height.
This style of chair is popularly associated
with Robert Manwaring, whose designs were
published in *The Cabinet and Chair-Maker's
Real Friend and Companion* (1765).

18th-century Venetian glass chandelier, thought
to have hung in Lord Burlington's Assembly
Rooms in York from 1730 until *c.*1840.

PICTURES

John Dryden, the Poet, holding a laurel wreath,
after Sir Godfrey Kneller's portrait in the
National Portrait Gallery.

Portrait of a Young Lady as Hebe,
by Richard Westall (1765–1836).

*A Virtuoso, holding a drawing, c.*1700,
by Willem Sonmans (1670s–1708).

Walnut veneered English
bidet, *c.*1730

The Queen's Room

This name derives from the visit by
Edward VII and Queen Alexandra (then
Prince and Princess of Wales) in June
1900. Green made relatively few alterations
to the early 18th-century interior apart
from introducing the present fireplace from
the adjacent Gray's Court in 1902. The
adzed floors, both here and in adjacent
rooms, were added in the 1920s.

Green always hung the walls with a Watts
damask fabric. At one time this extended
over the wooden dado, but by 1930 the
dado and the other woodwork had been
painted with the 'vermicelli' graining which
was reintroduced in 1996. In 1961 that
woodwork had been painted an off-white
colour and the damask replaced by the
flock paper which survives.

FURNITURE

Mirror in ebonised frame with gilt metal repoussé
mounts, English (?), *c.*1685.

Rosewood and brass inlaid commode, French, *c.*1730.

Carved and gilded figure, reputedly Charles II.

Mahogany wash-stand in the Chinese style, *c.*1760.

Carved and gilded slab table with marble top, English,
*c.*1725. The cipher in the frieze is that of James
Brydges, 1st Duke of Chandos.

Carved giltwood and gesso toilet mirror, English, *c.*1730.
The mirror plate and frame are not original.

Walnut veneered bidet, English, *c.*1730.

Pair of ebony, tortoiseshell and brass inlaid cabinets in the
manner of André Charles Boulle, French, *c.*1860.
Reputedly from the Hertford collection, part of which
now forms the Wallace Collection in London.

*Tester bed, c.*1740, from Houghton Hall, Norfolk,
much restored. The coat of arms is that of the Royal
House of Denmark (for Queen Alexandra).

Ebony and brass inlaid commode, French, *c.*1730.

Pair of carved giltwood stools, beechwood, English,
*c.*1705.

PICTURES

An Unknown Boy, attributed to Pieter Borsselaer
(1644–87).

An Unknown Young Man called the 'Duke of Argyll',
1702, by Thomas Murray (1663–1724).

Portrait of an Unknown Lady, English School, *c.*1670.

The Queen's Room

Princess Victoria's Room

Named after Edward VII's second daughter, who stayed here with her parents in 1900. The room retains its 17th-century ceiling and early 18th-century Venetian window. The adjacent north window was introduced by Green. The chimneypiece and pediments above the doors are from nearby Micklegate House. Green originally decorated the room with a matching fabric to the adjacent Queen's Room, but by 1910 it had been panelled and hung with tapestries. The present paint scheme, dating from 1994, restored that which had been introduced in the 1920s.

FURNITURE

Black stained chair with banister back, English, *c.*1710.

Louis XIV-style dressing-table with simulated metallic sphinx supports and marble and onyx top.

Beechwood and cane chair with moulded back, stained black, English, *c.*1715.

Oyster-veneered press, probably Dutch, *c.*1680. Olivewood and walnut.

Walnut and parcel-gilt slab table, English, *c.*1715, much cleaned, scraped and repolished.

Toilet mirror, of ivory veneers on a sandalwood carcase, Vizagapatam, south-east India, *c.*1780.

Stained beechwood and caned chair, English, *c.*1690.

Painted bureau, Italian, 19th-century. Decorated with a scene of Leda and the Swan after Boucher.

Boulle clock in the style of Louis XIV with a movement by Nicholas Fortin of Paris.

Carved walnut fire-screen with contemporary needlework, English, *c.*1695.

Walnut veneered folding writing-table, English, *c.*1690. The top is veneered with burr oak.

Carved giltwood and gesso pier-glass, English, *c.*1720.

*Tester bed, c.*1740, from Houghton Hall, Norfolk. Much restored with new hangings. The coat of arms is of Princess Victoria.

Two black painted stools, English, *c.*1705.

Walnut and cane chair with moulded back, English, *c.*1710.

PICTURES

Girl with tambourine (overmantel), English School, 18th-century.

Charles I, painted on glass, after the portrait by Edward Bower.

The royal visit in 1900

Princess Victoria's Room

The Tapestry Dressing Room

This room retains much of its 17th-century panelling, but it has been rearranged several times. Green removed a corridor and staircase soon after 1897 and then inserted another staircase in the north corner linking the Court Room below to the housemaids' rooms on the second floor. By the 1920s this had been replaced by a lift and bathroom in the two cupboards either side of the window overlooking Gray's Court. Green always claimed that not only the panelling but also the tapestries were found *in situ* behind later wallpaper.

Wax portraits of a Lady and Gentleman, *c.*1800 (Tapestry Dressing Room)

FURNITURE

17th-century Flemish verdure tapestries.

Leather-covered trunk, Spanish (?), 18th-century.

Backstool, perhaps French, mid-17th-century. Original cover.

*Stumpwork mirror, c.*1670.

Table, the top, drawer and sides English, *c.*1695, the legs and stretchers later.

Elbow chair, walnut frame, English, *c.*1740. The needlework cover is not original.

A joined oak chest, possibly Yorkshire, *c.*1670. From Heath Old Hall, the home of Frank Green's parents.

'Love seat' with walnut frame and needlework cover, English, *c.*1730.

Ivory crucifix in carved and gilt frame.

Stumpwork, 17th-century, representing the biblical story of Esther.

Armour, 17th-century.

Walnut veneered wardrobe, English, perhaps 1900, incorporating 17th-century elements.

Oak draw-leaf table, English or Dutch, mid-17th-century. The lunette carving on the rails is probably a later embellishment.

Bead basket, 17th-century, used to carry rosemary for guests at weddings and christenings.

(*Right*) The Tapestry Dressing Room

PICTURES

Portrait of a Lady, English, 17th-century.

Francis Drake (1696-1771), Yorkshire historian and author of *Eboracum,* by Nathan Drake, 1758.

Wax portraits of a Lady and Gentleman, English, c.1800.

Descend to the Hall and walk up the staircase at the far corner.

The Minstrels' Gallery

FURNITURE

17th-century lantern clock, possibly German, converted to pendulum. The thirteen-foot pendulum swings through a four-second cycle.

Two late 17th-century Indo-Portuguese ebony chairs.

PICTURES

Frank Green as a Young Man, by Prince Paul Troubetzkoy (1866–1938).

Portrait of an Unknown Man, by Henry Smith, 1844.

The King's Room *(illustrated on p.2)*

Although this is part of the earliest, 16th-century section of the house, the fireplace and cornice are 17th-century. Green introduced the mullioned-and-transomed windows and opened up the door through to the South Dressing Room. He originally painted the walls white, but by 1908 he had introduced the present stencilled scheme based on the 16th-century Painted Chamber in the nearby St William's College. The room was occupied by Edward VII in June 1900.

FURNITURE

Pair of ebonised cherrywood chairs, probably Dutch, early 19th-century. These are an imitation of 17th-century colonial ebony chairs.

Tester bed, early Georgian. Reputedly from Houghton Hall, Norfolk. The coat of arms is of the Prince of Wales.

Joined oak chest on stand, English, c.1690.

Carved giltwood elbow chair, French, c.1685, with cut velvet cover.

Japanned side-table, English, c.1690. The drawer and top are veneered with lacquer plates and the legs japanned to match.

Side-table of elm, stained black, English, 19th-century (?) in the style of c.1690.

Mirror, ebonised wood overlaid with repoussé gilt metal, English (?), c.1695.

Three beechwood stools, stained black, English, c.1705.

PICTURES

Portrait of a Lady, English School, c.1700.

Portrait of a Gentleman (thought by Green to be the novelist Fielding) in the manner of Thomas Hudson, c.1750.

17th-century stumpwork needlework in the Tapestry Dressing Room. It tells the Old Testament story of Esther, who interceded with the Persian King to prevent the massacre of the Jews

The Lobby

In the Lobby is a collection of mainly 18th-century drinking glasses.

The South Dressing Room

Green reduced this room to its present size by building the north-east wall. He again replaced 18th-century sashes with mullions and transoms and inserted the third window. Green originally decorated the room with a Watts wallpaper, but, some time before 1930, he introduced the current panelling, then painted green. This was painted over in 1970 but renewed by the Trust in 2003.

FURNITURE

Mahogany washstand, English, c.1780.

Pair of mahogany 'Hepplewhite' chairs, English, c.1785.

Gentleman's mahogany washstand, English, c.1770.

Early 20th-century travelling case, covered in black morocco with tortoiseshell fittings, some with Green's monogram, by Alfred Clark of London.

Oak gate-leg table, English, early 18th-century.

PICTURES

Lady Diana Manners as Queen Katherine in Henry V, by her mother, Violet, Duchess of Rutland, 1903. Lady Diana described Frank Green as 'our fairy godfather ... a big-fortuned eccentric who taught us about furniture and architecture and ornament'.

Portrait of a Dog, 'Frisk', by R.S. Moseley, 1875.

Mary Lycett, mother of Frank Green, by J.C. Moore, 1872.

Sir Edward Green (1831–1923) by J.R.G. Exley. After the death of his wife in 1902, Sir Edward lived with his younger son, Frank, at Treasurer's House until 1923.

Frank Green, by J. Percival Anderson, 1916

Frank Green in Hunting Pink, by J.R.G. Exley.

The Dining Room

This is part of the 16th-century section of the house. In the 18th century the panelling was introduced, and the ceiling embellished with fine plasterwork in an oval design incorporating the older crossbeams. It has been attributed to the Italian stuccoist Giuseppe Cortese. The chimneypiece is also 18th-century, but its overmantel was probably introduced by Green. He originally painted the panelling white, but the present graining was here by 1906.

FURNITURE

Set of six mahogany ladderback chairs, English, c.1745.

Carved pine slab table, English, c.1745. The present marble top is not original to the piece.

Inlaid display cabinet on stand. Possibly early 18th-century with a later stand. Contains Worcester porcelain.

Tripod table with carved dolphin supports and 'bluejohn' top, English, 19th-century, reconstructed from some earlier parts.

Mahogany display cabinet. A marriage – the upper part is a bookcase, c.1740, the lower part late 18th-century, cut down to fit. Contains a collection of mainly 18th-century Staffordshire and Yorkshire pottery.

PICTURES

Mr Halliwell, by Charles Towner, 1794.

Mrs Halliwell, by William Scott, 1840.

Mrs Edward Green (née Mary Ann Ironside), by Henry Pickersgill (1782–1875).

Flemish Landscape (overmantel), Flemish School, 17th-century.

Thomas Evans, by William Scott, 1840.

Edward Green, grandfather of Frank Green, founder of the family firm and inventor of the Economiser, by J.R.G. Exley, 1929, after Henry Pickersgill.

Thomas Green, father of Edward Green, by J.R.G. Exley, 1930, after Henry Pickersgill.

The Garden

The present design was formed by Frank Green in about 1900 from the separate plots of the three previous properties. He relied on a simple architectural layout and the contrast of grass, trees and old stone. The terrace walls contain architectural fragments from the many rebuildings of the Minster. When Green excavated the sunken lawn, he found so much old masonry that he concluded it must at one time have been used as the stonemason's yard for the Minster. The statues and wrought-iron gates were also introduced by Green. The pink sandstone figures are of Vulcan, Neptune and Ceres, while the lead statue of Mercury was adapted for use as a fountain.

Like the house itself, the garden owes its character to three elements – the close association with the Minster, the inspiration of the past, and the taste of an Edwardian connoisseur.

The statue of the goddess Fidelity with her dog in the garden

(*Left*) The garden front

(*Opposite*) The Dining Room

The Medieval Treasurers of York Minster

The site of Treasurer's House is an ancient one, going back – or, more literally, down – to the Romans. This part of York is built on Roman foundations: behind the house the city walls still follow the line of the Roman fortress, while in front York Minster stands on the site of the legionary headquarters. In the cellars of the house itself the base of a Roman column and a section of Roman road were discovered when the house was restored in 1897, and further discoveries were made in the 1950s. Roman evidence of a rather different sort allows the house to claim the oldest ghosts in the country. In 1953 an apprentice plumber working in the basement claimed to have seen a bedraggled troop of Roman legionaries coming through the wall – at the level, unknown to him, of the original Roman road.

The history of the house really begins with the medieval Treasurers of York Minster, the first of whom was appointed in 1091. It is to this period, when the Church was such a power in the land, that Treasurer's House owes its secluded setting, looking out over the cathedral close of York Minster. In the Middle Ages the Minster precincts were completely sealed off from the city (hence the word 'close'). Only four gates allowed access to this exclusive domain of the Church – the sole survivor is now the National Trust shop in Goodramgate. Within these boundaries everything lay under the jurisdiction of the Minster clergy, amongst whom the Treasurer was second only to the Dean in wealth and power.

St William of York, Treasurer from *c*.1113 to 1143, is depicted in many of the Minster's stained-glass windows and is commemorated by the nearby St William's College

The medieval Treasurers were not given a great mansion just because of their high status. The Treasurer, then as now, controlled the finances of the Minster, but it was also one of his responsibilities to entertain important guests of the Minster, and for this he needed a large residence. Other duties included looking after the magnificent treasures of the great church (most were later to be melted down on Henry VIII's orders during the Reformation) and paying for the labour and materials needed to run the Minster from day to day.

The holders of the office included members of the royal family, the younger sons of powerful barons and Italian papal nominees who probably never set foot in England, let alone York. They would enjoy the rich revenues, while a sub-Treasurer was appointed to do the work. In the few manuscripts that survive from those days there is an occasional glimpse of the Treasurer's status: the will of one dated 1509 shows he was rich enough to leave each of his 38 menservants a bed – a rare luxury at a time when most people slept on benches or on the floor.

Little is known of the original Treasurer's House. A 12th-century external wall survives intact on the inside of the neighbouring Gray's Court, and much medieval masonry remains in the basement of Treasurer's House, but this is quite likely to be stone that was later reused.

Only the name survived, long after the Treasurers themselves had disappeared, to remind us of a very different way of life around the Minster.

A page from the 1510 inventory of York Minster's treasures, which were the responsibility of the Treasurer

The History of the House, 1547–1700

The Parliamentary general
Thomas Fairfax owned
Treasurer's House in the
mid-17th century

17th-century stained glass
in the Hall

The Reformation of the English Church meant the end of the medieval world of the Treasurers. The brief announcement of the abolition of the office issued in 1547 by the last Treasurer, William Cliff – 'The treasure having been confiscated there is no further need of a Treasurer' – has often been interpreted as a laconic epitaph for the medieval Church. But it is more likely that the removal of the treasure was being used as an excuse to seize the Treasurer's endowment. William Cliff, like many churchmen, was handsomely rewarded for surrendering without a fuss, being appointed Dean of Chester. The post of Treasurer of York Minster was not revived until 1936.

After being seized by the Crown, Treasurer's House was owned by two post-Reformation Archbishops before it became the property of a third, Thomas Young, Archbishop of York from 1562 to 1568. Young was an important and active political figure. As Lord President of the Council of the North, he was responsible for enforcing Queen Elizabeth's government and policing the still insecure Protestant Church throughout the North of England. He was also notorious for enriching himself at the expense of the Church and for pulling down much of the Archbishop's Palace, of which only the chapel (now the Minster Library) and an arcade still stand in Dean's Park. This may have been both the source of the stone and the reason for building a new residence: the present Treasurer's House.

Certainly, the architectural structure of the house owes more to Young and his descendants, who owned the house until 1648, than to any later owners. The earliest part of the house was probably built in the 16th century on the traditional pattern of a central hall with two end sections, one for services and the other for private living. Within a few decades, however, the house was almost completely rebuilt by the Youngs. Early in the 17th century the central block was widened, the lower wing extended, and the upper one completely rebuilt. The arrival of Renaissance ideas in England made an impressive symmetrical front fashionable, and this is clearly what the owner and his builder were trying to achieve. But although at first sight the garden façade gives an impression of symmetry, it is fairly easy to see that not only do the windows vary, but, more fundamentally, the floor levels of the south-east (right-hand) wing are lower than those of the central block and north-west (left-hand) wing. For the present garden façade was superimposed on the asymmetrical earlier building in order to form the balanced composition we see today.

The Youngs did not enjoy their new mansion for long. In 1617 the Archbishop's son, Sir George, was able to entertain King James I at Treasurer's House, but by the time of Charles I's execution in 1649 Sir George's grandson had had to sell. Treasurer's House passed through many hands. On occasion the ripples of history eddied into the backwater of Minster Yard: one of the first owners after the departure of the Youngs was the great Parliamentarian leader Thomas Fairfax, who may have added the Long Gallery at the back of the house (now part of Gray's Court).

The superficially symmetrical façade was imposed on the rambling old building in the early 17th century

The 18th and 19th Centuries

In 1720 Elizabeth Montagu, wit, writer and literary hostess, was born at Treasurer's House, while it was from an upper window in the winter of 1782 that John Goodricke, the deaf astronomer, observed the orbit of the star Algol, 'and thus laid the foundations of modern measurement of the universe'.

During the 18th century Treasurer's House became the residence of gentry families, lawyers and clerics. This was a time when the intellectual and cultural life of provincial cities like York was thriving, and the local landowning gentry kept up a town house where they spent much of the winter away from the mud and boredom of the country.

Although structurally unaltered, much refitting of the house was carried out during Georgian times. In 1698 Robert Squire bought the house and sufficiently altered it for Drake's *History of York* to say 40 years later that he had rebuilt it. Squire's work may have included new panelling and converting the windows from stone mullions and transoms to wooden sliding sashes. In the 1720s and 1730s the fine staircase and Venetian windows were added to the north-west wing, perhaps by Elizabeth Montagu's father, Matthew Robinson.

The most far-reaching change made to the house during this period was its division in 1725, when Bacon Morritt bought part of it from Matthew Robinson.

The Dining Room, with its fine plasterwork ceiling attributed to Giuseppe Cortese, was fitted out by the Morritt family, who owned this part of the old mansion (the 'Little House') until 1813.

Other owners who may have contributed to the 18th-century alterations were Canon Edward Finch, and the rabidly anti-Jacobite Dr Jacques Sterne, whose nephew Laurence wrote the novel *Tristram Shandy*. Over the years further divisions were created, extensions and outbuildings were added to the different properties, and the house began to go down the social scale.

By the end of the 19th century the house was in a state of decayed gentility, a quality shared by its inhabitants. Sir George Young's original mansion was divided into at least five separate properties, occupied by a medley of genteel spinsters and widows, a doctor, a music teacher and Edwin Gray, a York solicitor whose family owned the back of the house for over a century.

In 1897 one of these properties was put up for auction: it was bought by Frank Green. Within six months he had bought out three more of the owners and by 1900 he and Edwin Gray had created from the warren of intersecting properties two separate and self-contained residences – the present Treasurer's House and Gray's Court. A new phase in the history of the house had arrived.

Treasurer's House around 1800, when it still had its 18th-century sash-windows (later removed by Frank Green)

The astronomer John Goodricke, who first observed the orbit of the star Algol from a window of Treasurer's House in 1782

Frank Green

A Family Business

Frank Green was the grandson of a successful engineer and industrialist from Wakefield. In 1845 his grandfather, Edward Green, had invented 'Green's Fuel Economiser', a device which used the waste gases from a steam boiler to pre-heat water fed into it, thus saving energy and cutting costs dramatically. In the great age of steam power the Economiser was an enormous success and made Edward Green – known as 'Old Neddy' to his workforce – the fortune that was to save Treasurer's House.

The next generation decided to improve the family's social status. Old Neddy's son, another Edward – inevitably known as 'Young Neddy' – had married Mary Lycett, the daughter of a Cheshire vicar from a rather more genteel family than the newly rich Greens. According to family tradition, it was she who determined that the profits of industry should support a more gentlemanly way of life.

On Old Neddy's death, Young Neddy and his wife leased a dilapidated, but romantic, country mansion near Wakefield, Heath Old Hall, attributed to the great Elizabethan architect Robert Smythson. Later they bought a town house in London, and Edward Green, elected as Conservative MP for Wakefield in 1885, was rewarded with a baronetcy in the following year. But above all it was sporting life – foxhunting and shooting – which gave the Greens an entrée into the social élite.

Young Neddy, or Sir Edward as he was soon to become, was an astute businessman and an autocratic employer. He took a typically direct route to the top by buying a shooting estate in Norfolk adjoining Sandringham, the country residence of the Prince of Wales (later Edward VII). Here he built Ken Hill, a country house in the avant-garde 'Queen Anne' style, and on its completion in 1880 had the satisfaction of seeing the Visitors' Book begin with the names of the Prince of Wales and his son.

This was the start of much royal patronage of the Greens, notably the royal visit to Treasurer's House in June 1900. But the path of social advancement never ran entirely smoothly. The most spectacular royal connection of all was the Royal Baccarat Scandal of 1890, in which the Prince of Wales and Sir Edward's elder son Lycett were both involved. Lycett accused one of the Prince's friends of cheating at Baccarat during a house party at Tranby Croft near Hull. In the publicity surrounding the ensuing court case, the Greens were dragged through the mud as newly rich upstarts.

It was in this atmosphere that Frank Green, the younger son of Sir Edward, grew up: a late Victorian melting-pot, in which entrepreneurial energy, sporting enthusiasm, advanced aesthetic tastes and some tension over social origins were all combined. Frank and his elder brother were sent to Eton and Harrow respectively, Frank going on to Oxford. Unlike his handsome, self-assured brother, Frank was shy and diffident as a young man, with the hot temper of the over-sensitive (as a boy he once felled his tutor with a cricket bat). While Lycett was intended to lead the life of a country gentleman and devoted most of his energies to hunting, Frank was designated to take over the family business.

Green's Economiser Works, Wakefield – the source of the family's wealth. Frank Green described himself, only half in jest, as 'the industrious apprentice', who slaved in the muck and grime so that the rest of the family could enjoy their lives of leisure

The programme for a fête given for the children of the workers at the Greens' Wakefield factory

(*Opposite*) Frank Green with his father, Sir Edward, in hunting pink on the steps of Treasurer's House

Elaborate arrangements were made for the visit of the Prince and Princess of Wales in 1900

George V and Queen Mary studying a model of Green's Economiser in 1912. When the King asked what came out of it, he was told, 'Fox-hunting and champagne, Your Majesty!'

Rediscovering the Past

Not that it was all work. Frank himself never married and could afford to indulge expensive tastes. He was a bit of a dandy, always immaculately turned out and impeccably dressed. In later life he invariably sported a floppy silk bow tie and a dazzling array of gorgeous waistcoats, natty shoes and hats. He was a very particular man, always insistent on absolute cleanliness and tidiness. There are still notice-boards at Treasurer's House with careful instructions for the staff, and for the benefit of the housemaids he had studs fixed in the floor to mark the exact position where furniture should stand.

Frank Green was equally fussy over his creature comforts. He was fond of fine foods: his groceries were sent up from London and he imported a French chef to cook for him at Treasurer's House. While York was good enough for the staff laundry, his own was sent down to London every week by train, and it is said that he slept in fresh Jaeger linen sheets every night of his life. One former kitchenmaid remembered that he used to come down at night to inspect the kitchen and turn out drawers he did not consider tidy enough.

Much of this might suggest the ostentatious leisured lifestyle of the rich in Edwardian times, but Frank Green had a more serious side. His mother had superintended the restoration of Heath Old Hall and had imported fashionable designers and artists to work there and at Ken Hill. Frank seems to have derived his artistic interests from her and was already a notable collector of antiques when he bought Treasurer's House. Indeed it seems

Frank Green was always immaculately turned out

26

likely that one reason for the purchase was the need to house his collection.

Frank Green's rescue of Treasurer's House was also part of a much wider rediscovery of the past, of which other symptoms were the success of the magazine *Country Life* and the foundation of the National Trust itself in 1895. Frank Green did not merely choose a 'period' residence, but carefully restored it to what he thought was its original appearance, removing all 19th-century alterations and additions. He set out the rooms as a sequence of 'period settings', incorporating features from different periods of the house's history, with appropriate antique furnishings in a way that sought to be both authentic and imaginative. He even wrote a guidebook to his home, stressing its medieval origins and the succession of period styles it exhibited.

The years between 1897 and 1914, when Frank Green restored and lived at Treasurer's House, were the heyday of the Greens. The company was booming, the family united; Frank gave magnificent parties at Treasurer's House and built up his collection in a torrent of acquisitions and disposals.

After the Great War, and Sir Edward's death in 1923, Frank himself was reaching retirement age. However, he remained Chairman of the Company and refused to relinquish complete control. This led to a bitter family dispute in the early '30s, and those members of the family who took sides against him set up a rival company. Many years before, Frank had decided to leave Yorkshire. In July 1930 he gave Treasurer's House and its contents to the National Trust and moved to Dulverton in Somerset, where tales are still told of his generosity, eccentricity and extravagant whims. He died in 1954 at the age of 93, an Edwardian who had long outlived his time.

Frank Green with the staff of Treasurer's House in the 1920s. The women flanking him later became the first curators of the house for the National Trust

Restoring Treasurer's House

The main work of restoration by Frank Green and his architect, Temple Moore, was to sweep away all the extensions, outbuildings and partitions that had been added in the 19th century and which completely obscured the great 17th-century house of the Youngs. According to Temple Moore's daughter, the house was little more than a 'bug-ridden slum' when her father started work. Temple Moore had trained under George Gilbert Scott the Younger and his original work – mostly churches in the North of England – was in the high-minded tradition of the Gothic Revival. His other speciality was restoration work: Temple Moore was responsible for the recovery of St William's College nearby, which Frank Green also owned, and the neighbouring Gray's Court, as well as much other sensitive work in the city.

In returning the house to its original 17th-century shape and dimensions, much of its history was revealed. Most prominently perhaps, the remains of the original mullion-and-transom windows, which had been replaced by sash-windows in the 18th century, were discovered. From this evidence Green and Temple Moore made the major decision to restore the original 17th-century windows – though not always in their 17th-century positions.

The most dramatic changes inside were made to the central block of the house. Green seems to have believed that the central body of the house had been a medieval great hall, and that when the Youngs had rebuilt the house in the 17th-

Green and his architect, Temple Moore, restored the original 17th-century mullion-and-transom windows

century, they had *lowered* the floor to fit in an upper floor. Green therefore had Temple Moore pull all this out to make the whole central block into one enormous space, retaining only the half-timbered gallery supported by a line of classical columns. Most modern opinion holds that this part of the building dates from no earlier than *c.*1560. But whatever the case, we can now appreciate the work of Green and his architect without worrying too much about its authenticity. In fact it is precisely those rooms which are most fictitious, such as the Great Hall and the Drawing Room, that are the most exciting spaces in the house.

The main phase of the restoration, comprising structural repair, the reinstatement of the garden front and the creation of the Great Hall, was complete by June 1900, in time for the royal visit by the Prince and Princess of Wales (later Edward VII and Queen Alexandra) and their daughter Princess Victoria. It was in their honour that the King's Room, Queen's Room and Princess Victoria's Room were so named.

After this initial period of collaboration with Temple Moore, Frank Green continued the development of the house on his own. Although he was nowhere else as creatively ambitious as in the Great Hall, he treated the rest of the house in much the same way – as an architectural framework on which he would build up his idea of a historic house.

Green removed floors and ceilings to re-create what he believed had once been the medieval Hall. Photographed by Bedford Lemere in 1902

Creating the Period Rooms

The fire-screen in Princess Victoria's Room is decorated with English needlework of *c*.1695, showing the contemporary method of displaying porcelain on brackets

English needlework of *c*.1725 covers the set of walnut chairs in the Blue Drawing Room

(*Opposite*) Green introduced this stencilling to the King's Room

The creation of period settings was the main theme Green followed in the arrangement of the house. The names different rooms were given at various times strongly emphasise this 'period' theme: Restoration Room, Tudor Dressing Room, Queen Anne Drawing Room, Georgian Bedroom, William and Mary Staircase, Chippendale Bedroom, Sheraton Room, Vanbrugh Room. In part this succession of historic interiors must have been dictated by the need to accommodate his extensive collection of furniture. But it was also conditioned by the house itself – Frank Green's correspondence and notes show that at a very early stage he had the idea of setting out the rooms to illustrate each period of the history of the property. Green was one of the first to appreciate that a historic interior was a totality in which architecture, decoration and contents all combined to form a satisfying whole.

Another feature typical of advanced contemporary taste was Green's concern for texture and pattern. The best example of this interest is Green's unusual appreciation of historic textiles, tapestries and needlework. New fabrics were also based on old examples at Knole and Hardwick, and were supplied by Bodley, Garner & Scott (later Watts & Co.), a firm which Temple Moore's old master had helped set up specifically to provide needlework, textiles and wallpaper for historically minded architects. A director of the firm, J.L. Davenport, apparently suggested much of the interior decoration. Green later replaced many of these Watts papers with panelling, but one has been restored during the recent redecoration.

The adzed floors in the bedrooms of the 'Queen's side' (north-west wing) are further evidence of this concern for texture, above and beyond the mere reproduction of an antique effect. The boards of these floors have been worked with the old-fashioned carpenter's adze, instead of being planed, thus giving the characteristic scooped and scalloped surface.

The whole creation of the house was a constant process of accretion. The adzed floors, like the stencilled walls of the Entrance Hall, were introduced only in the 1920s, shortly before Green moved to Somerset. Similarly, comparison of his guidebooks, inventories and early photographs shows an enormous turnover of furniture and decoration in his 30 or so years of ownership. This is best exemplified by the West Sitting Room.

The house was never very 'lived in' – perhaps inevitably in the absence of a wife and family. One might almost say that it was Frank Green's hobby, to be played with, rather than a home. He even admitted it was not 'an ideal residence' in a letter to the *Yorkshire Herald* about the preservation of York's architectural heritage. Instead, the house was always intended to be something of a showpiece. Press reports of the royal visit in 1900 stated that the house could be visited by 'special permission', and Green himself issued guidebooks in 1906, 1908 and 1910. He commissioned the photographer Bedford Lemere to produce a permanent record of his creation, and there were illustrated articles on the house in *Country Life* in 1906 and 1922. The final demonstration of his care for the house came in 1930, when he gave Treasurer's House and its contents to the Trust.

The Collection

The late 17th-century longcase clock, made by Ben Merriman of London, in the Entrance Hall

This walnut cabinet in the Court Room was illustrated in Percy Macquoid's *History of English Furniture*

Antique-collecting was in the air at the end of the 19th century, as nostalgia for a stately past took hold and the art of making furniture declined. Great inherited collections of antique furniture had long been treasured by the aristocracy, and on occasion particularly rare or splendid pieces had been collected by individuals with antiquarian interests. However, it was only in the late 19th century that a specifically historical approach became established. At this time more comprehensive collections of English furniture were systematically built up, often by newly rich businessmen like the industrialist Viscount Leverhulme and the newspaper magnate Randolph Hearst.

At the same time the first proper histories of English furniture were being written, above all Percy Macquoid's *History of English Furniture* (1904–8) in four monumental volumes. Macquoid was the other English pioneer in deliberately setting out rooms of different periods in one house, and they almost certainly knew each other well. Many of Green's pieces were used to illustrate the *History of English Furniture*, and there is even a family tradition that it was he who persuaded Macquoid to write his work.

Green seems to have specialised initially in walnut furniture of the late 17th and 18th centuries, and this period is still well represented at Treasurer's House. Together with Macquoid and a handful of other collectors, he had a pioneer interest in 18th-century furniture at a time when reproduction Chippendale and Sheraton furniture was popular, but the real thing was generally unregarded.

In particular, Frank Green was one of the very first to appreciate the importance of original and period fabrics. He discovered historic upholstery beneath later re-coverings on several pieces he bought, such as the needlework love-seat and armchair in the Tapestry Room.

Green bought widely – through dealers, at public auctions and by private sales from country houses – and sold almost as often as he bought. The range and styles of furniture he acquired became increasingly diverse and included Boulle (inlaid brass and tortoise-shell) furniture and many ebonised, japanned, gilded, stained or otherwise 'disguised' pieces. In his later years Green also specialised in late 18th-century satinwood furniture. At least one room was once furnished in the Sheraton style, but very few pieces from this period now survive in the house.

Treasurer's House is not a museum of the finest specimens of antique furniture: there are some outstanding pieces, but equally there are some over-restored and altered ones and 19th-century copies 'in the style of ...'. Essentially, it is an imaginative re-creation of an historic interior according to the taste of an Edwardian connoisseur, and the interest of the collection is inseparable from its setting. Both remain very much as they were created by Frank Green in the early 20th century.